Love to Color

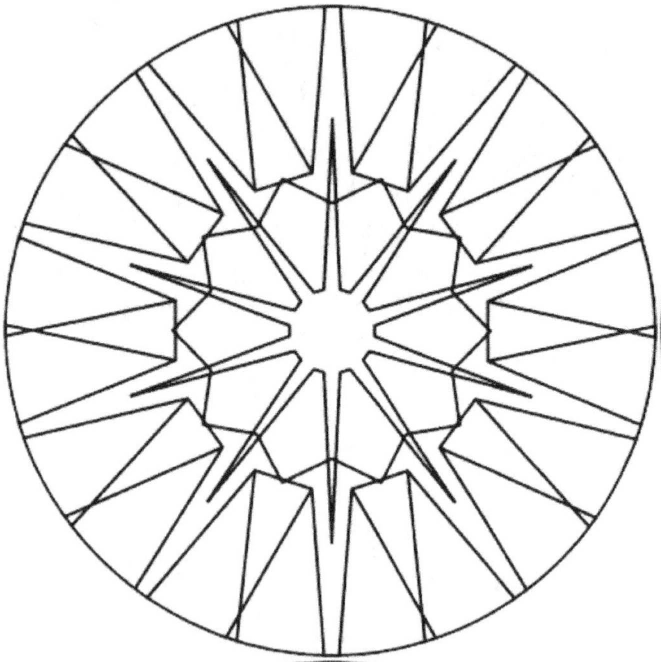
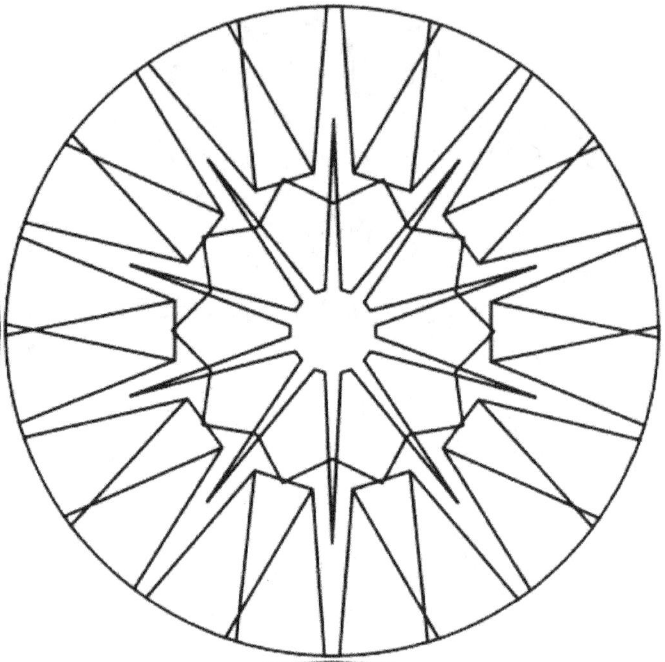
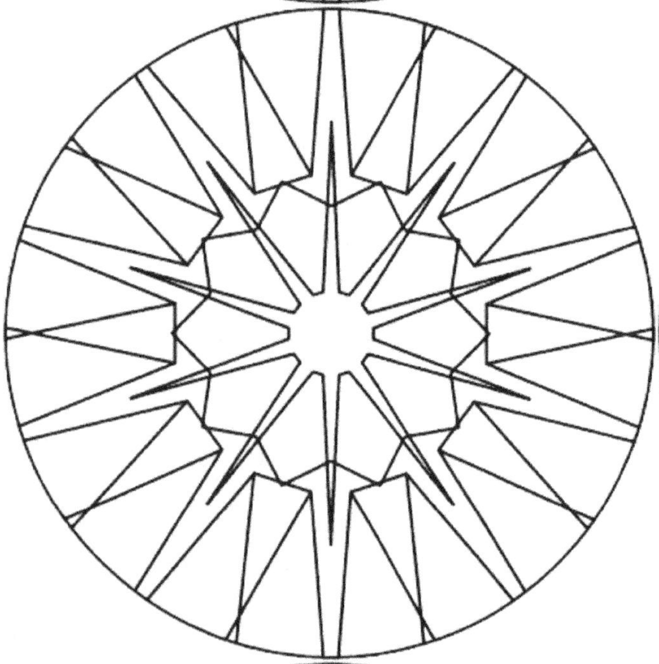
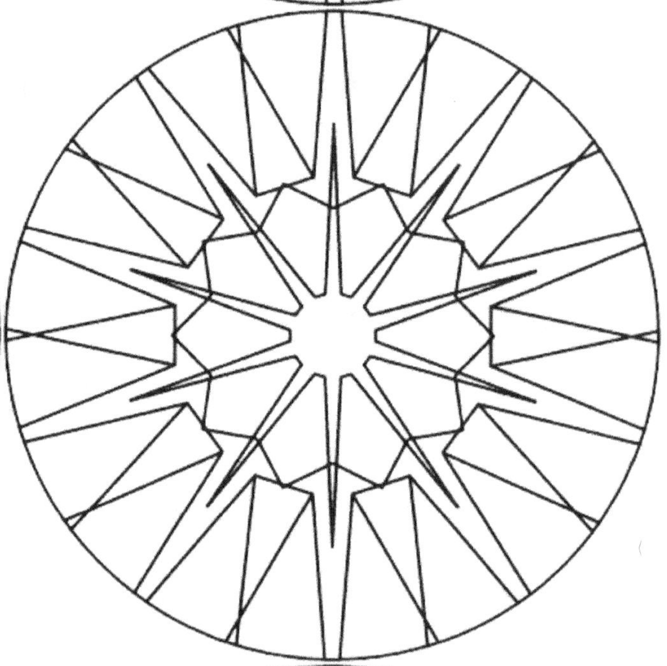
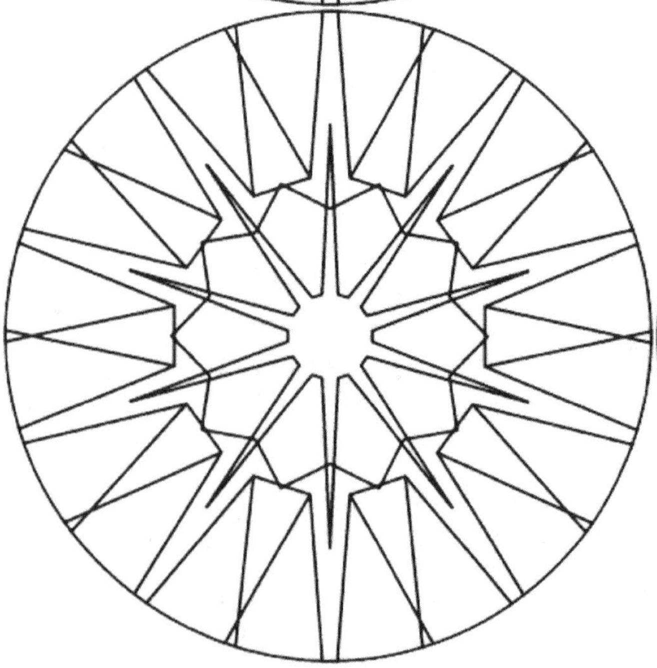
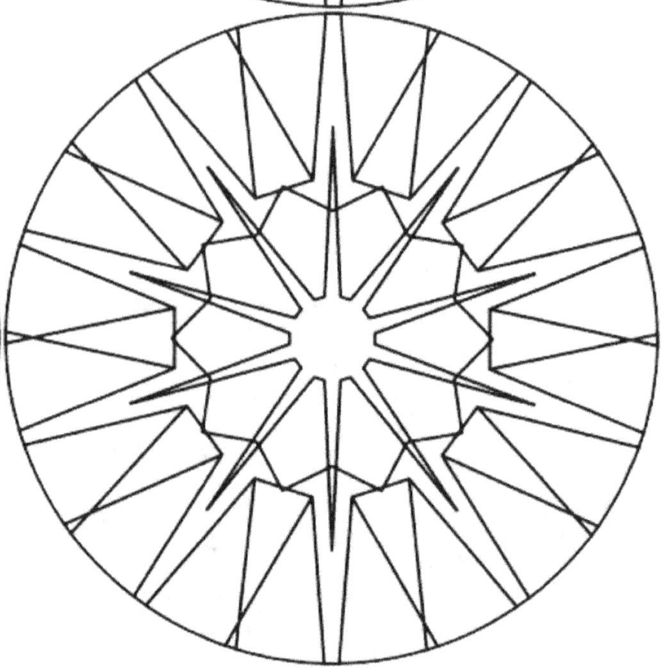

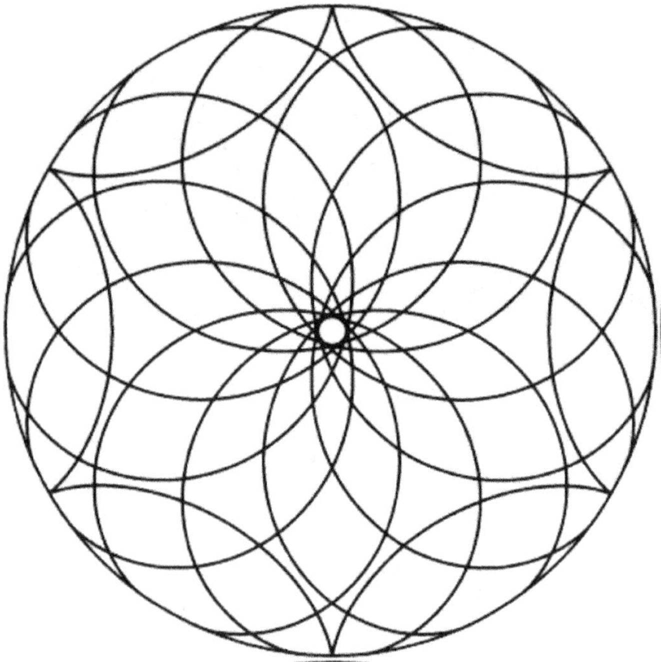
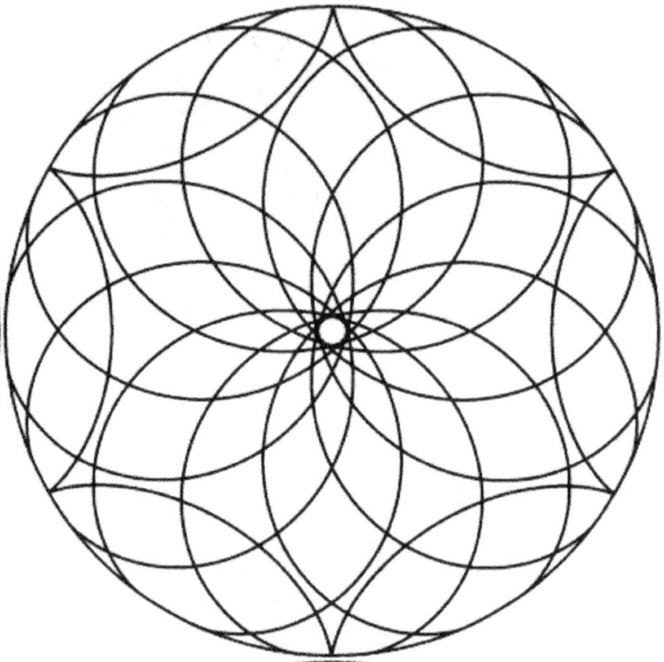

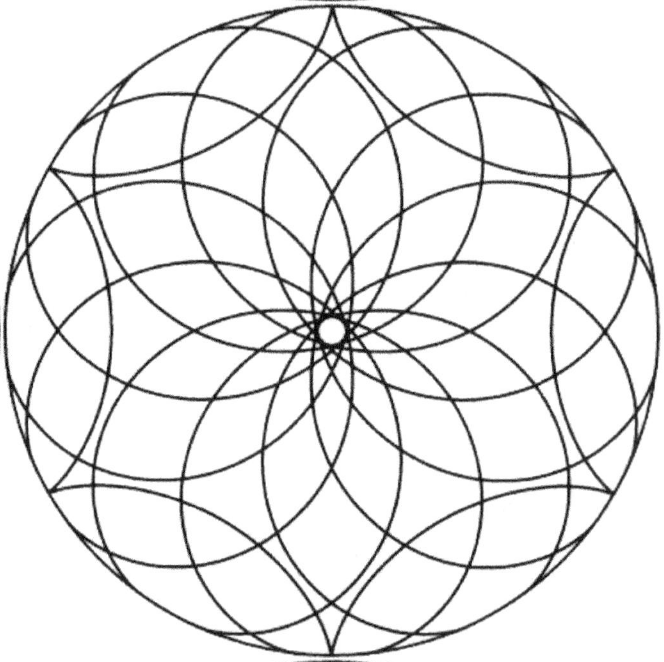

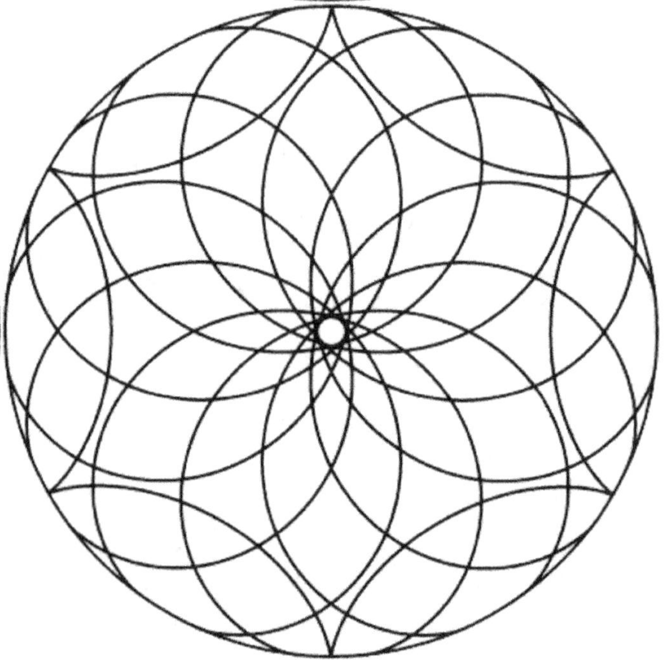

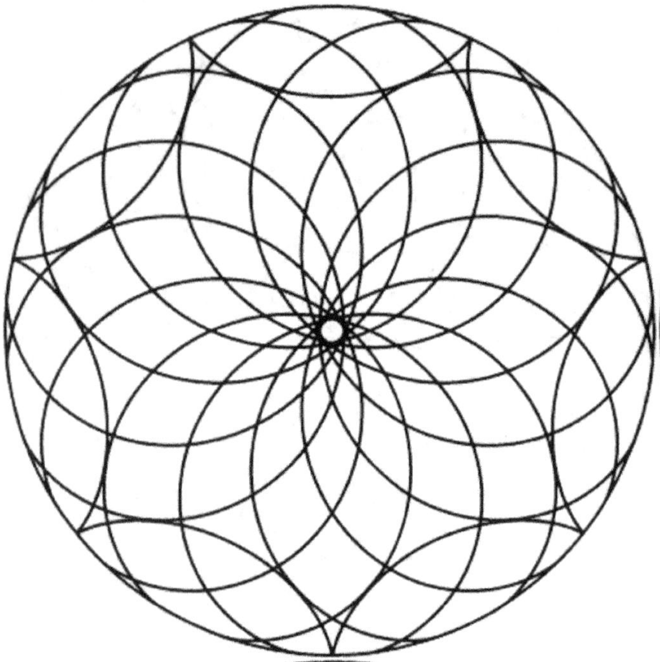
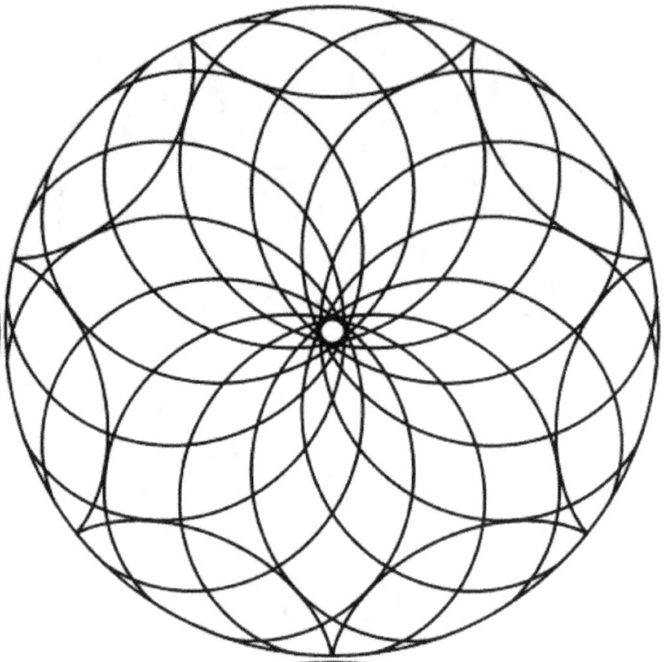
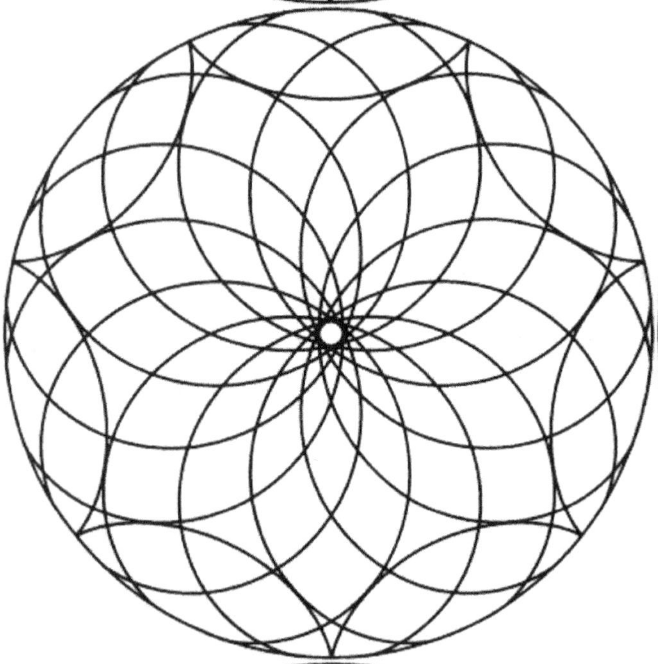
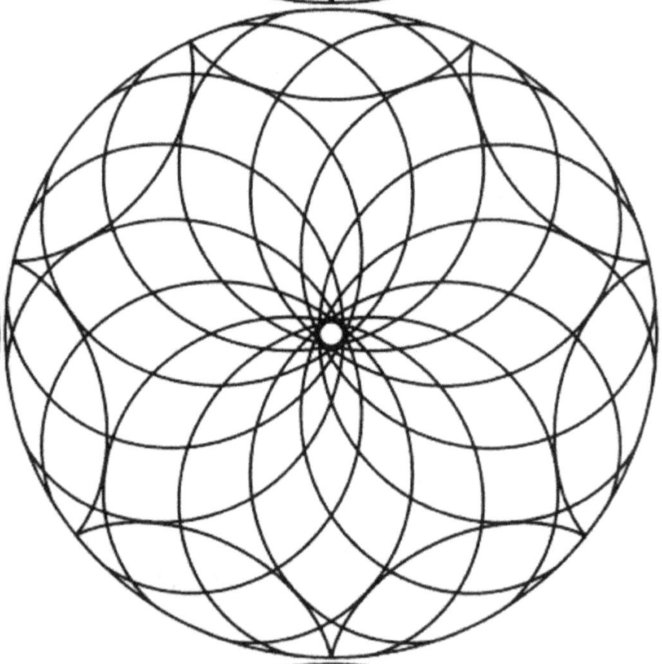
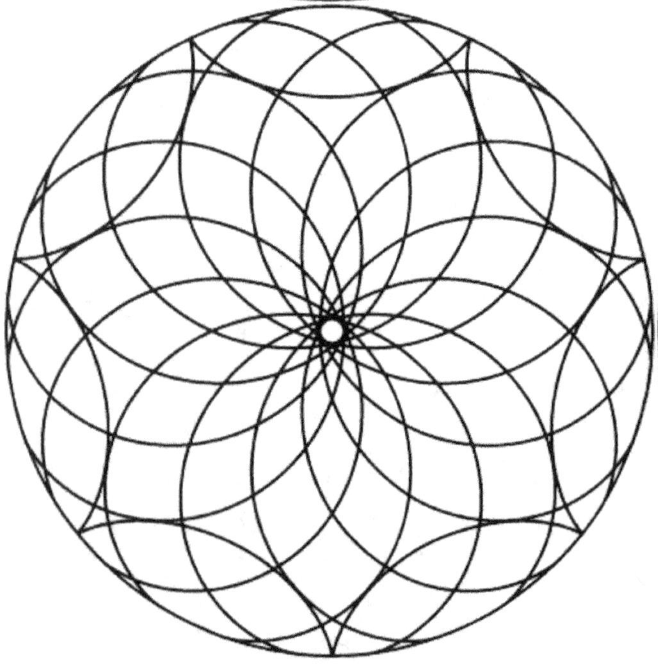
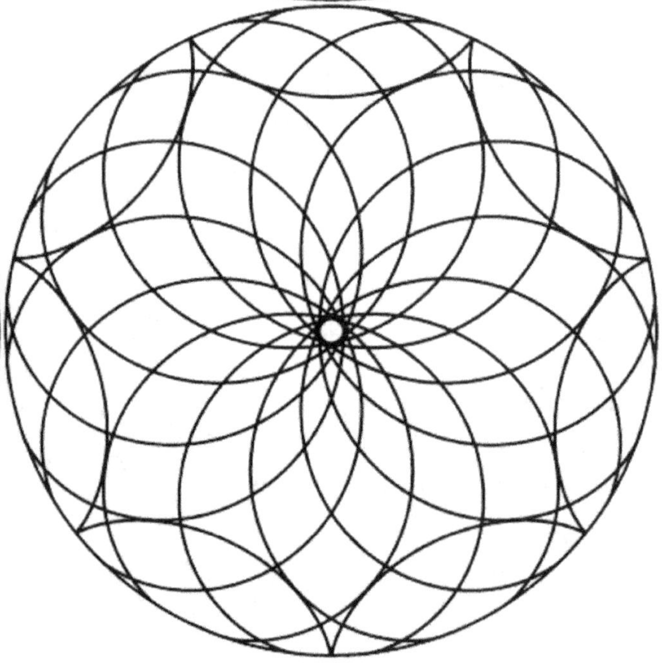

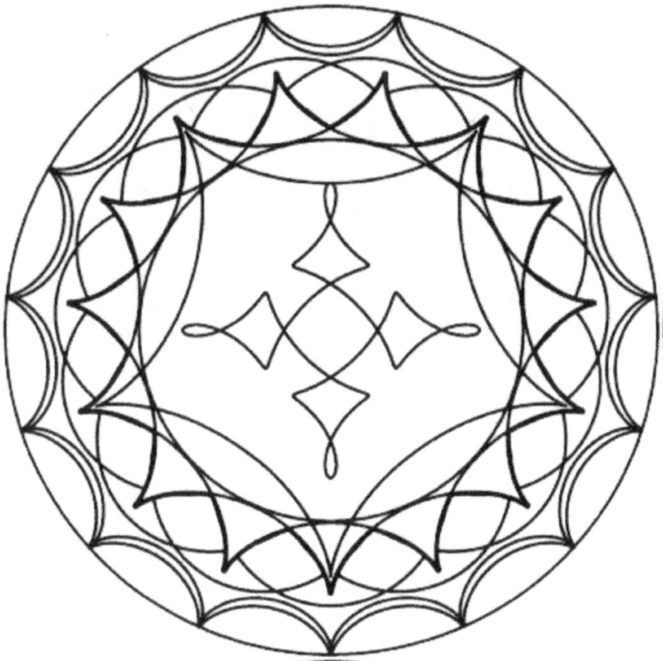
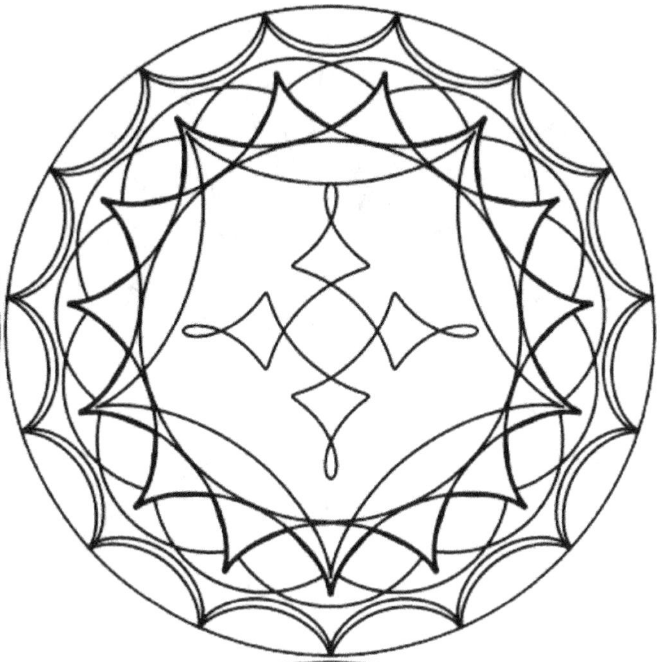
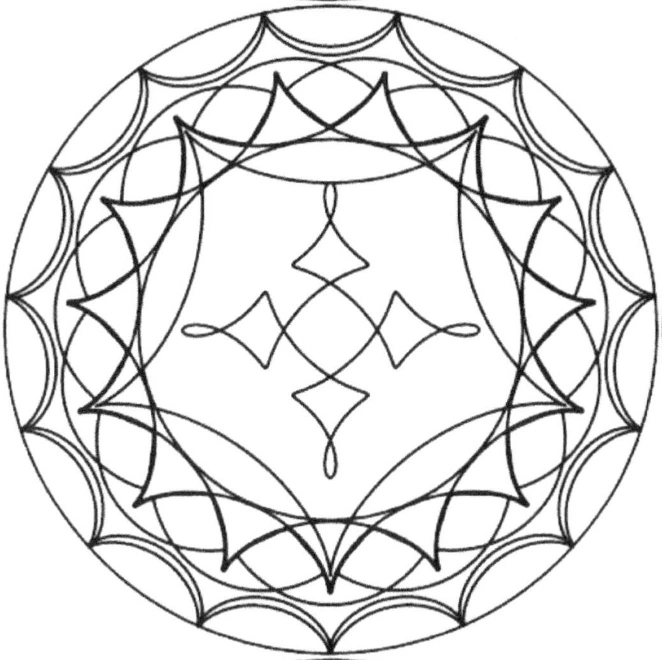
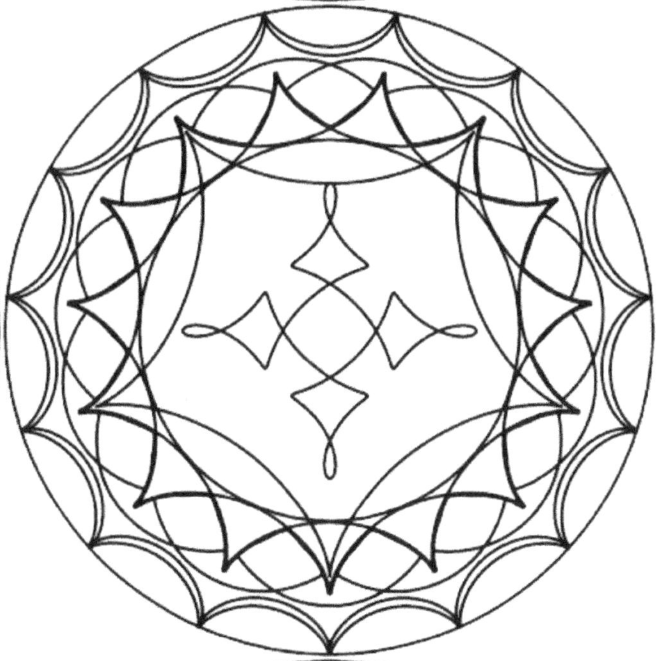
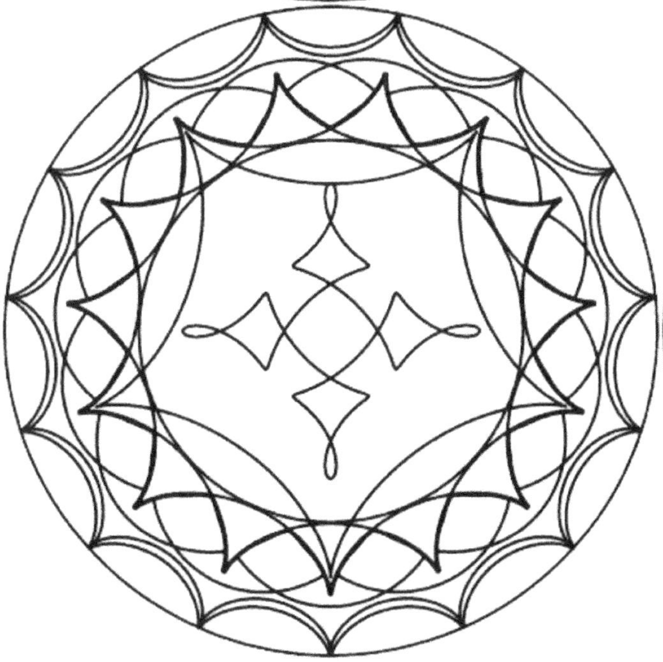
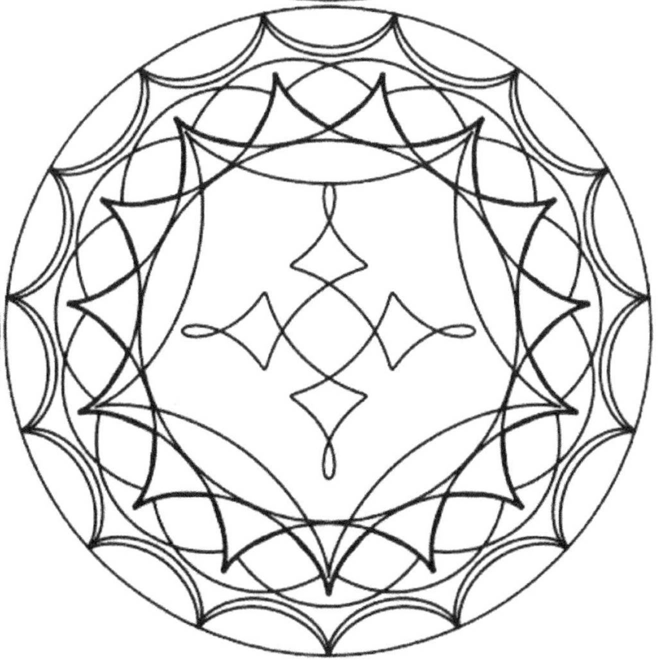

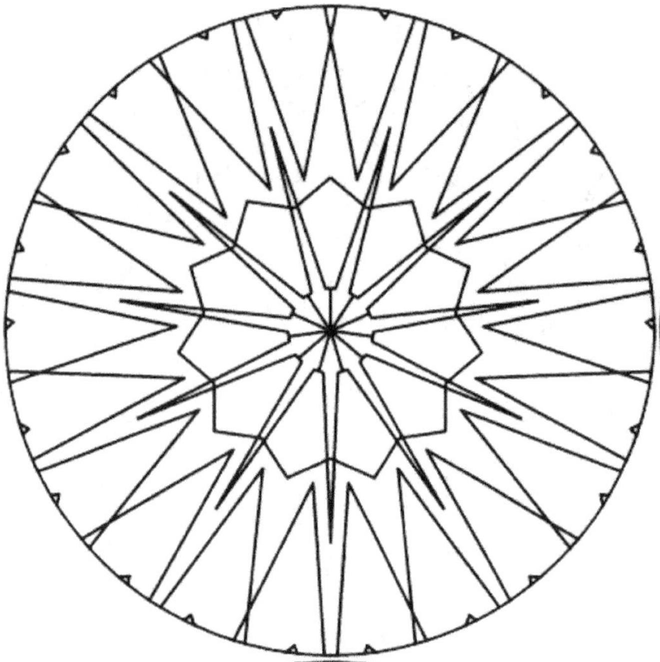
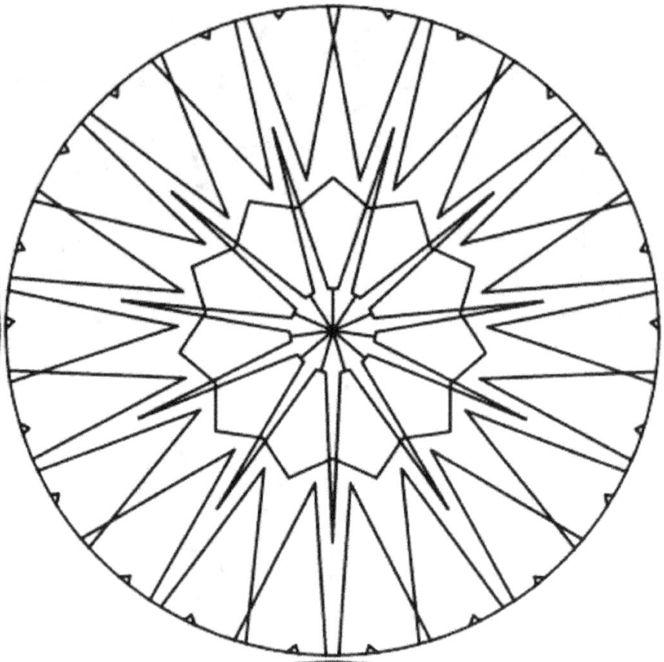
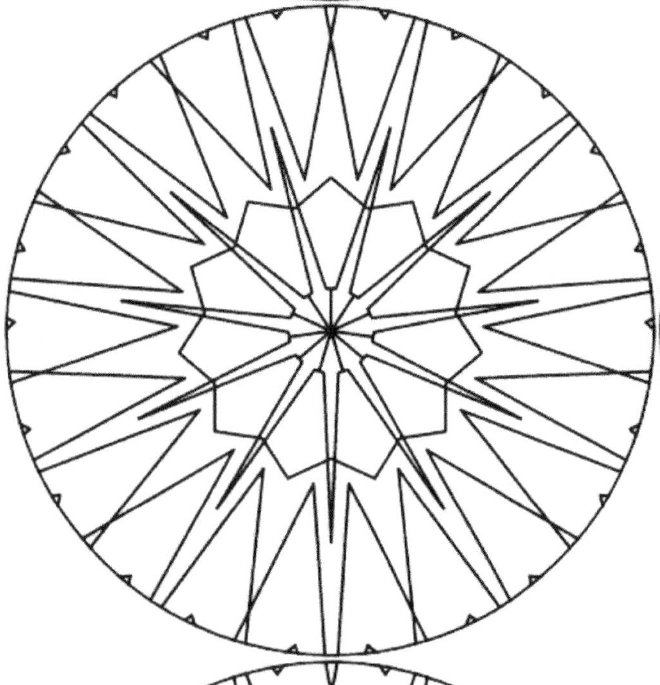
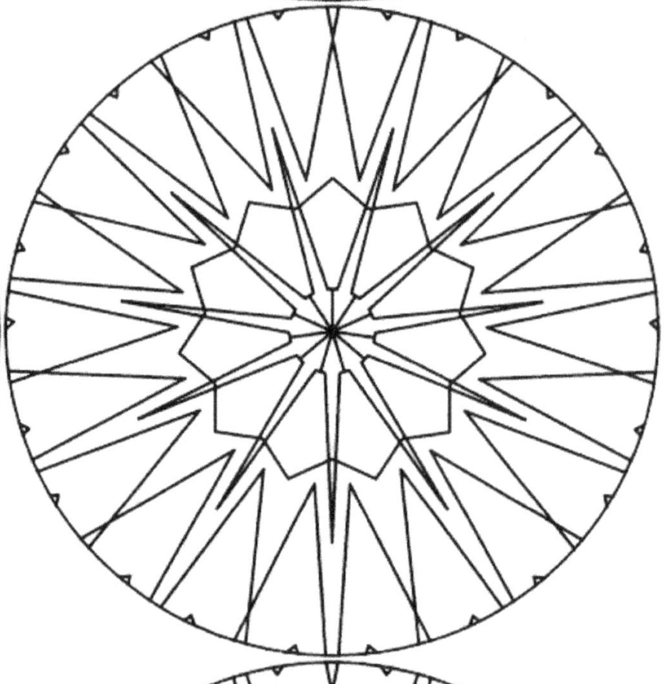

www.ingramcontent.com/pod-product-compliance
Lightning Source LLC
Chambersburg PA
CBHW081755280526
45789CB00008B/2859
9781541023895